Jarrold Bird Series Book 4
with text by **Reg Jones**

Birds of the Mountains and Moorlands

Jarrold Colour Publications, Norwich

Introduction

A line drawn on a map from Bristol to the mouth of the Tees divides mainland Britain into two quite different parts. The land to the east is largely low and flat, whilst that to the west is higher ground which includes mountains ascending to 3,000 or 4,000 ft.

Mountain tops are regions of extreme exposure. Temperatures tend to be low and frosts are intense and frequent. The rainfall is usually heavy and wind speeds are characteristically high. Under such conditions the soil often amounts to little more than rocky fragments. Not surprisingly the vegetation is sparse and plants which are present are low growing and well anchored. There is little to attract birds and, in Britain, only a very few feed and breed at, or near to, the summits. These are the dotterel and the snow-bunting, with ptarmigan on the higher slopes. Other birds, mainly predators, nest amongst the high crags and this group includes the golden eagle, the peregrine falcon, the raven and the buzzard.

Below the summits there is usually an area of inhospitable country, wild and uninhabited, and generally referred to as moorland. The soil is acidic, often very wet, and not suitable for cultivation. Peat accumulates, but the nature of the area can vary and moorland takes on a number of different forms. By far the most familiar is heather-moor, the type most people visualise when the term moorland is used.

Heather-moors occur where there is a slope which promotes drainage. They are drier than other types of moorland and commoner on the eastern sides of our mountains where the rainfall is lower. Naturally heather is the dominant plant but others, like bilberry and crowberry, grow in the shade of the heather and they are important because of their berries which are much valued by some birds. Undoubtedly the most characteristic bird of heather-moor is the red grouse. It feeds mainly on the young shoots of heather and this accounts for the frequent burning of moors so that the subsequent regeneration from both roots and blown seeds will produce an abundance of new and succulent growth. Heather-moors are managed so that grouse may enjoy the best possible conditions. But other birds are present. Meadow pipits are abundant and, when considering all types of moorland, the commonest species. They are accompanied by skylarks and, when the heather is particularly rank, by twites. Merlins, our smallest falcons, feed largely on meadow pipits, and, when tolerated by keepers, are heather-moor residents. So too are hen-harriers when they are not molested, but the commonest predator is the kestrel which normally feeds on small mammals.

The dampness of many moorlands is probably the reason why the bird population includes several waders, and although heather-moor is one of

the drier types it often includes wetter areas where the ground is broken and the peat exposed. In such situations, and at around 1,500 ft, the golden plover nests together with the 'plover's page', the dunlin.

Grassland moors vary enormously in their composition. On the flat tops of the Pennines there are often extensive stretches of cotton grass growing on a thick layer of wet peat. On gentle slopes with relatively soggy and acidic soil there is wet mountain grassland which, in the drier parts may merge into heather or, if grazing is heavy, into upland pasture with silver hair grass and fescues. None of these is so rich in birds as heather-moor. Meadow pipits and skylarks persist but there are few red grouse. On the other hand, black grouse may flourish on some grassland moors. Of the waders, the curlew is most characteristic and in recent years it has been joined by the redshank.

Moorlands are rarely uniform. They are dissected by deep clefts, punctured by pools and tarns. These clefts, referred to locally by such terms as gills, are often steep-sided and are the favourite haunt of the mountain blackbird or ring ouzel. If a mountain stream issues from the cleft, grey wagtails will haunt its banks, dippers explore its waters and common sandpipers nest amongst the boulders and gravel by the water's edge. Sandpipers will also be found by moorland tarns, being joined in some places by gulls, especially black-headed gulls.

The Curlew is our largest wader and, in spring, no sound is more typical of moorland than the bubbling trill it produces during its display flight. As the bird glides over its territory the song begins as a slowly repeated liquid note which, gradually increasing both in pace and volume, reaches the trill as a great crescendo to which no other adjective is more appropriate than bubbling. The other characteristic call issued in flight is a loud 'cooor-wi'.

Some curlews are present around the coast at all seasons. Many winter in Ireland or in southern Europe, but mature birds are back on their nesting grounds by late February or early March. Although found on heather-moors they probably prefer grass-moors and rough pasture, especially when there are wetter patches, at elevations between 500 and 1,000 ft. Some, however, may nest at higher levels, others in quite low-lying meadows. Whilst on their nesting grounds, curlews feed on worms and grubs, often obtained by probing in soft earth with their long bills.

As with many other waders, the normal clutch is four, the darkly marked greenish-brown eggs being laid in a simple hollow lined with grasses or sprigs of heather. They are incubated for four weeks and the chicks, after drying off, leave the nest almost immediately. Although many early clutches are lost to carrion crows, young birds and parents are ready to leave their breeding haunts in late July or early August.

Golden Plovers generally breed at higher levels than curlews and are probably more typical of heather-moors. They favour ground where the

Below left:
Curlew (×¼).
Right: *Golden Plover, southern race in spring (×½).*

peat is exposed and broken, and the vegetation short as, for example, after burning. Nests consist of scrapes lined with a few strands of heather and, like the curlew, four eggs are usual, the ground colour being buff and blotched with dark markings.

The golden plover is so named because its upper-parts are spangled gold and black. Birds nesting in Britain are members of a southern race which, in spring, have the breast and belly black in colour whilst the face is dusky. In the northern form, which breeds in arctic Europe, the face is as black as the breast and there is a prominent white band separating the upper and lower parts. Both types lose their dark colouration in winter and are indistinguishable, the under-parts becoming pale with soft golden mottlings.

Outside the breeding season golden plovers form flocks which haunt pastures and stubbles, often in company with peewits. They feed mainly on insects and worms, spiders and snails picked up from the soil's surface. It is probable that many British breeders winter in this country but some may reach as far south as the Mediterranean.

Early in the year compact companies of golden plovers begin to move northwards and, as they pass overhead, it is possible to hear their musical liquid flight call 'tlui'. They are back on their nesting grounds by March to indulge in extravagant displays before eggs are laid in late April or May.

Dunlins nest on elevated moorland reaching, on occasion, even higher levels than the golden plover. They are more characteristic of grass-moors, the nest being enclosed within a tussock, and usually placed not far from a pool or tarn. The distribution is not uniform. A few may breed in Wales but the species becomes more common on moving north through the Pennines into Scotland.

In winter, the dunlin is usually the commonest of our shore birds. Most of these will breed to the north of Britain. In spring, birds migrating from southern Europe and Africa will form the British nesting population, arriving at their breeding areas towards the end of May. At this time they are trim little birds, 7 in. long, chestnut streaked black above, light below with a black patch on the lower breast.

Left: *Dunlin* (×¾).
Above right:
*Common
Sandpiper* (×½).

The Common Sandpiper haunts the banks of clear flowing moorland and mountain streams, together with those of lochs and tarns. Running over the shingle or flitting from stone to stone it snatches up small aquatic organisms. Each pause is characterised by a typical bobbing action but when disturbed it flies in a manner quite distinct from other waders. It sweeps low over the water with a flicking flight, flickering wing beats alternating with short glides as the wings are held rigid at the bottom of a down beat. The alarm note is a shrill 'twee-wee-wee'.

Common sandpipers are olive-brown flecked with darker marks above, pure white below except that their necks bear brownish streaks. They are summer visitors nesting in suitable country from Wales northwards. Arriving on the south coast during April and May the majority then progress along a westerly route to their breeding grounds. Here the males display in the air with ascending spiral song flights and on the ground with typical wader-type bowings and wing raisings. The song is generally described 'kitti-weewit, kitti-weewit'. By the end of May or early in June, four eggs are laid in a nest which is on the ground and often close to the water. It is a simple hollow, usually sheltered by vegetation. Eggs are incubated for three weeks and, since the chicks are independent after a further four or five weeks, nesting areas are abandoned in July. British birds probably winter for the most part in Africa or southern Asia.

The Greenshank is much scarcer and more restricted in its range than those waders already mentioned. It is confined to moorland which generally includes swampy areas and small lochs beside which the bird can feed. In Britain it nests regularly in the central and northern highlands of Scotland; in Lewis and Harris, but much less frequently in Skye and the Inner Hebrides.

Greenshanks are summer visitors which winter in tropical and sub-tropical areas of the Old World. They arrive from mid-March onwards and are seen first around the coast, recognisable from the more common redshanks by their larger size and greyer plumage. The legs, of course, are greenish in colour and, in flight, there is no white bar on the wing, although a prominent wedge of whiteness on the body is apparent when the wings are extended.

A greenshank's nest is a shallow scrape made on the ground by the hen. Very often it is adjacent to some prominent local feature such as a rock or fragment of bleached timber. Four eggs are laid early in May and both parents share the incubation, events then following the usual wader pattern. Small parties start moving southwards in late July, often using inland routes, stopping at sewage farms, by tidal estuaries or similar places where there is the opportunity to look for food in shallow water.

Four other common waders which are not specifically associated with moorland must be noted. In the lowlands Redshanks frequent riverside meadows and grassy marshes, but in Scotland and the Pennines they are regular summer residents on higher ground, hiding their eggs in the grassy tussocks of rough upland pasture. They are rarer in the Welsh hills, absent in Devon and Cornwall. Lapwings, widely distributed, also nest on upland pasture but choose ground with shorter grass than the redshanks.

Left: *Greenshank* (×½). **Above:** *Redshank* (×⅓).

Snipe are present, too, favouring wetter areas with patches of rushes and sedges. In those places where efforts have been made to drain the land the number of snipe has declined, but the bird is still common up to 1,000 ft or more on suitable ground from the West Country to the north of Scotland.

The majority of Oystercatchers breed around the coast. In Scotland they have long been known to nest far inland along the shingly banks of rivers and streams, finally reaching lochs at 1,500 ft. This tendency to penetrate inland has spread further south and in post-war years oystercatchers have been frequent nesting birds by moorland streams in northern England. The trend has not yet reached Wales.

The Dotterel is unlike the other waders in that it is confined to the barren plateaux of the higher mountains. In Scotland it nests at over 3,000 ft in the Grampians and, perhaps, a few peaks in the Western Highlands, but at a lower level in at least one place in north-western England.

Dotterels winter in North Africa and as far to the east as Persia. They arrive in Britain about the end of April and make the passage northwards in small parties, or 'trips', keeping to high and wet inland areas rather than the

Above: *Oystercatcher* ($\times\frac{1}{4}$). **Above right:** *Dotterel* ($\times\frac{3}{7}$).

coast. At this time they are in their breeding plumage which shows two bands of white, the first running above each eye with the right and left halves meeting at the back of the head to form a 'V', the other across the breast and separating the chestnut-coloured belly from the darker feathers of the lower neck. They are small birds, only slightly larger than dunlins.

On the breeding grounds the normal roles of the sexes are reversed. Once a clutch of eggs is laid, it is the male which is responsible for most of the incubation. Additionally the hen takes the principal role in the display which precedes egg laying. A special feature of dotterels is their extraordinary tameness. When sitting on eggs, a bird can often be approached to within a few feet and this trusting nature is probably the reason why they are now restricted in Britain to the highest and most remote regions.

Wagtails are small slender birds, always on the move, their long tails constantly quivering. In the air, their progression is distinctly undulating. Never clad in sombre colours, they are always eye-catching. Insects and their larvae form the major part of their food.

The Grey Wagtail is the species especially typical of mountain and moorlands. It haunts upland streams, particularly if they are fast flowing and shallow with plenty of stones and rocks between which it can flight. On the shore it runs nimbly over the wet gravel, pausing to snatch grubs and snails or to dart upwards and take an insect on the wing.

In appearance, the grey wagtail is bluish grey above with light under-parts, pale yellow on the belly but citron-yellow at the base of the tail. The throat of the male is black in summer, the hen's remaining light.

Grey wagtails nest on ledges or in clefts on the banks of streams, especially where the flow is greatest. Starting in late April, usually two broods are reared. The majority of birds leave the hill country in autumn to winter on lower ground and a few may emigrate southwards.

Although the Pied Wagtail is frequently found near water its range is wider than that of the grey. It is often present on upland pastures, snapping up insects disturbed by grazing cattle or sheep. In such situations it will nest in recesses within dry stone walls or similar sheltered places.

The pied wagtail is the British form of the White Wagtail, a species which inhabits most of Europe and Asia. It is not easy, at all seasons, to distinguish the pied from the other races of white wagtail, the only constant difference being the colour of the rump which is black in the pied, grey in other forms.

Yellow Wagtails are summer visitors reaching no further north than southern Scotland. They spend the winter in tropical climates. In Britain, their favourite habitat is wet pasture and whilst they are not typical of mountains or moorlands they are often present at lower altitudes where mountain streams flow through squelching meadows. The nest is always on the ground.

Like the pied wagtail, the yellow wagtail is only one form of a larger group. There are several races in Europe. All have yellow under-parts but, in the males, whereas the British race's head is yellowish green, that in Central Europe is blue-grey. The hens are duller and more difficult to distinguish.

Meadow Pipits are not unlike skylarks in their general colouration, being brown above with darker markings and lighter below with dark streaks. They are smaller, rather less than 6 in. in length, have no crests and differ in their behaviour. The cock's song flight consists of a steep ascent followed by a more gentle descent with wings extended and tail spread, but the height reached is less than that achieved by the skylark, rarely exceeding 100 ft, and the song is thin and feeble.

Meadow pipits are typical of open country, breeding throughout Britain in both rough grassland and heather-moor. The nest is on the ground and hidden beneath a tuft of heather or grassy tussock. Eggs are laid from late April onwards and, following this early

Above: *Yellow Wagtail* ($\times \frac{2}{3}$). **Top of page:** *Pied Wagtail* ($\times \frac{2}{3}$). **On facing page:** *Grey Wagtail* ($\times \frac{1}{2}$).

start, it is usual for two broods to be reared. In the late summer they desert the moors and move to lower-lying land. British summer residents probably winter in south-west Europe whilst birds from further north, Iceland and the Faeroes, pass the colder months in this country.

Cuckoos deposit their eggs more frequently in the nests of meadow pipits than of any other species. On moorland, the majority of cuckoos are reared in this way.

Meadow pipits live almost entirely on insects and other small creatures but Twites, being finches, feed mainly on seeds. By no means as abundant as meadow pipits, they nest in small colonies, generally in rank heather, from the Pennines northwards to the Scottish Highlands and Islands.

Twites are not very striking birds. Buffish brown above with darker streaks, the breast is lighter but still darkly marked. About the same size as its commoner relative, the linnet, it lacks the red crown and breast. There is a slight pink tinge on the cock's rump but this is not easily seen.

As with meadow pipits, twites leave the moorland in autumn. They are partial migrants, some wandering as far as the Mediterranean in winter.

Above: *Meadow Pipit* ($\times\frac{1}{2}$).

One other small bird, the Snow Bunting, is peculiar to the mountains. Only a very small number nest high in the Cairngorms amongst the loose rocks and screes. When flying, they appear predominantly white and are said to resemble snowflakes. In summer they feed on insects but wintering on the coast, seeds make up the major part of their diet.

Wheatears are characteristic of barren places like rocky hillsides or upland pastures. They are summer residents and among the first migrants to arrive in spring, the earliest making their appearance about mid-March. Widely distributed, they move northwards along the east and west coasts before striking inland to their final destinations. They are unmistakable. Flitting low over open country, ever restless, the white rump at the base of the tail identifies the species.

The sexes are well defined. The cock has light grey upper-parts with a black stripe below the eye and dark wings.

Above: *Cock Snow Bunting in summer* ($\times\frac{1}{3}$). **Top of page:** *Twite* ($\times1$).

The tail bears central and terminal bands of black whilst the under-parts are white yet tinged with sandy yellow below the beak. In the female, the tones are more subdued with brown above and buff below, but the white rump remains.

Whilst favouring open ground, wheatears seek out protective cavities for roosting and nesting. Simple nests constructed of grasses, lined with hair, may be built in a hole in the ground, a rabbit burrow, or in some crevice within a stone wall. Usually about six eggs are laid which hatch in a fortnight, after which the young are reared on an insect diet. Prey is snatched from the ground and sometimes, in order to survey the field, wheatears hover like kestrels at a height of six to ten feet before diving to take beetles or grass-hoppers.

Early to arrive, they are among the first to leave, migrating southwards from mid-July along a route which leads to tropical Africa and Arabia.

Except during the severest winters, Dippers are resident by clear moor-land streams. They are very territorially conscious, each pair covering a length of about a mile. When disturbed, a bird will fly fast and low, up or

down stream, uttering a tingling 'clink'. It alights on a stone and bobs spasmodically, which movement is responsible for the name – dipper. Stockily built and about the size of a thrush, it often cocks its tail and very much resembles its relative, the wren. It differs in being dark in colour, almost black, except for the white breast with a chestnut band on the lower margin.

Dippers obtain much of their food from the stream's bed. Sometimes a bird will wade, but often it plunges beneath the surface of the water and remains submerged for about a quarter of a minute, clinging to stones whilst searching for insect larvae, snails and freshwater shrimps.

Nests are always built by the water. Suitable sites are used with some regularity. They may be crevices within banks or ledges beneath bridges. The nest is globular with a side entrance, in form very like a wren's.

On lowland streams dippers start their courtship early in the year and the first eggs are produced in March. At higher levels where nesting can occur at over 2,000 ft, these events take place about a month later and so the frequency of double broods is reduced. Young birds are not great travellers

Left: *Cock Wheatear* ($\times\frac{1}{3}$). **Above:** *Dipper* ($\times\frac{1}{2}$).

and tend to establish themselves within a radius of a few miles from where they were hatched.

In Britain the Ring Ouzel, or mountain blackbird, tends to replace the common blackbird at elevations above 1,000 ft. At such heights it is more characteristic of moorland than of mountains and, in particular, of the steep-sided clefts and gorges through which flow moorland streams. Here, in spring, it constructs blackbird-like nests on rocky ledges or on banks overhung by heather or grass.

On the Continent ring ouzels are rarely found below 3,000 ft. They frequent open coniferous woodland and secrete their nests within the various kinds of conifers.

Ring ouzels winter around the Mediterranean. The Atlas Mountains are said to be one of their great strongholds. They move northwards in spring, some coming to Britain, others to Scandinavia, the Pyrenees, the Alps and mountainous regions as far to the east as those adjacent to the Caspian Sea. During migration they can be seen in open country, very like blackbirds in appearance but distinguished by the white crescents on their breasts.

Ring ouzels start nesting in April and often two broods are reared. When hatched, the chicks are fed on worms and grubs, much in the manner of other thrushes. Later in the summer when small flocks form in anticipation of their autumnal exodus, moorland fruits such as bilberry and crowberry are enjoyed.

Grouse are plump birds with relatively short yet broad wings, living for the most part on plants such as heather. They are of circumpolar distribution in the northern hemisphere.

Over much of northern Europe and Asia, the Willow Grouse is the lowland representative of the grouse family, but in Britain it is replaced by its close relation, the Red Grouse, which is quite specific to this country. In particular, it is the most characteristic bird of heather-moors where it is resident throughout the year.

The red grouse derives its name from the subdued rufous colour of the body. The wings and tail are darker, and over the eye is a red wattle. When disturbed, it takes off with whirring wing beats low over the heather and, before alighting, the flight ends in a shallow glide. A cock grouse is a noisy bird. Its call is a loud, quickly repeated 'kowk-owk', whilst on its own territory its challenge is 'go-back, go-back, go-back, back, back'.

Above left: *Cock Ring Ouzel* ($\times\frac{3}{7}$). **Above:** *Red Grouse* ($\times\frac{1}{7}$).

Above: *Cock Ptarmigan* ($\times\frac{1}{6}$).
Right: *Blackcock* ($\times\frac{1}{5}$).

At higher levels, about 2,000 ft, in the Scottish Highlands the red grouse is succeeded by the Ptarmigan. It is found beyond the tree line where the terrain is rocky and the vegetation includes much moss and lichen.

Ptarmigan resemble willow grouse. In summer, the body and breast are grey-brown, the wings and belly being pure white. The sexes may be distinguished by the warmer body colour of the hen. Both have wattles, but they are more pronounced in the cock.

Living at high altitudes and often in close proximity to snow, ptarmigan resemble other arctic species by changing colour in winter. Both sexes become white except for the black sides to the tail.

Like the red grouse, flights are usually of short duration, spells of rapid wing beats alternating with glides. Ptarmigan do not migrate but, in the autumn, form packs or coveys which may move to lower ground in hard weather when snow makes feeding difficult.

In spring both red grouse and ptarmigan use display grounds where cocks may perform their annual rituals, but these are not so renowned as those of a third species, the Black Grouse.

Black grouse are found on moorland and particularly if adjacent to woodland which is thinning out into scrub. The male, the Blackcock, is glossy black with a lyre-shaped tail. There is a white wing bar best seen in flight. The female, the Greyhen, is similar to a red grouse but larger, with less rufous, whilst the broad tail is only slightly forked.

Early in the morning in springtime, black grouse congregate at well established gathering grounds, referred to as 'leks', for competitive display and for courtship. Here the cocks make the most of themselves. First they raise their widespread tails to expose the fluffy whiteness beneath, and with drooping wings and distended wattles, each bird patrols a part of the lek, leaping into the air from time to time and emitting a hissing challenge. Inevitably birds meet in confrontation. Puffing themselves up, they make intimidatory charges which are often inconclusive. Sometimes, after a clash of breasts, one bird achieves clear dominance. Between these bouts of activity the blackcock squats on the ground and, quivering with excitement, croons 'kroo-kroo-kroo', a song which attracts the greyhens in the vicinity. Tentatively a greyhen enters the lek and, in due course, mating occurs.

Eggs are laid in a scrape amongst the ground cover. Incubation and the care of the young rests entirely with the greyhen, the family remaining together until late in the year.

The Short-eared Owl, or Moor Owl, flies by day. Longer winged than most other owls its flight appears almost leisurely as it floats on slow wing beats of great amplitude. Flapping flight is interrupted from time to time by spells of gliding during which the wings are held rigid above the body so as to form a shallow 'V'. It quarters moorland and at a distance is easily confused

with a harrier, but at closer range the blunt rounded head shows it to be an owl.

When displaying in spring, it indulges in circling, vertical flights. It calls 'boo-boo-boo'. Suddenly it loses height and while doing so claps its wings several times below the body. If its territory is entered, it is fearless in its dive bombing.

Short-eared owls feed mainly on small mammals, especially field voles, and the number of owls in an area is very much related to the size of the vole population. On moorland, nests consist of rough scrapes amongst the heather or rough grass. Increasingly, nesting takes place in young forestry plantations. Clutches of four to seven white eggs are laid, but there may be more in good vole years. At the nest it is possible to see the bird's special features, the striking yellow eyes, the upper-parts warm brown and mottled with buff. The ear tufts are not particularly discernible unless the bird is alarmed.

Short-eared owls nest from the Pennines northwards through Scotland. Some are present at all seasons but there is an element of autumnal migration southwards.

Falcons have narrow pointed wings and tapering tails. Their flight is swift and direct. Three species are associated with moorlands and mountains: the merlin, the kestrel and the peregrine falcon.

The Merlin is the smallest of our native falcons. Neither male nor female exceeds 12 in. in length and, as in most birds of prey, the hen, referred to as the falcon, is the larger. The cock, or tiercel, is dark blue-grey above, warm buff below and streaked with brown. The grey tail bears a terminal band of black. In the female, the back is dusky brown and the tail is barred, whilst the ground colour of the under-parts is almost white.

In the breeding season merlins are encountered on heather-moors where

Above left: *Short-eared Owl* (×¼). **Above:** *Hen Merlin* (×⅓).

they feed largely on small birds such as meadow pipits. These are taken in flight. Hunting takes the form of a breathless pursuit, the bird skimming and swerving over the heather giving chase to its prey. Hovering and stooping are rarely practised.

A merlin's nest is a simple scrape on the ground amongst the heather. Sometimes eggs may be laid on a rocky ledge or in an old nest left in a wind-swept tree from a previous year. Chicks hatch towards the end of June and, at first, are brooded and tended by the hen whilst the cock hunts for food which is brought to a plucking site, generally an elevated knoll not far from the nest, where it is decapitated and plucked. The tiercel calls 'quee-eep' to attract the female which quickly transfers the food to the nest where it is dispensed a morsel at a time. Only when the chicks are large enough to be left with safety do both birds hunt, and then prey is deposited at the nest unplucked for the youngsters to deal with. Young birds fly when about four weeks old.

Most merlins do not spend the winter in moorland country. Many move to the coast but some may reach the Mediterranean and beyond.

Above: *Hen Kestrel* ($\times\frac{1}{5}$). **Above right:** *Peregrine Falcon* ($\times\frac{1}{3}$).

Heather-moors are managed so that grouse may flourish. To this end, in the past, merlins have all too frequently been relentlessly shot and this probably accounts for their scarcity in many places. Kestrels are usually the commonest falcons seen over moorland. Perhaps they are tolerated because they feed, in the main, not on birds but on small mammals, field mice and voles, taken on the ground after being sighted from the air by a hovering bird. This capacity for hovering is the characteristic which makes them so easily recognisable. They are not so agile as typical falcons and seldom take food on the wing.

Kestrels are widespread in their distribution, as common over lowland grazing marshes as upland moors. Except in the extreme north, they are present at all seasons although there is some small autumnal dispersal.

The Peregrine Falcon is the largest falcon breeding in Britain, the female being about 18 in. in length. In the air, it is a typical falcon; the long wings sweeping backwards to a point, the tail short and tapering. It shows marvellous agility and speed. Prey is taken on the wing, relatively large birds like pigeons and ducks being struck down, slashed by the talons, at the end of a magnificent stoop during which the hunter plunges earthwards, with wings almost closed. It is a spectacular performance.

Peregrines nest on inaccessible rocky ledges in wild hill country. Here, at close quarters, it is possible to note the black moustachial stripe, the dark upper-parts, and the light buff feathers below.

Once nesting is finished, peregrines are wanderers. They may be found in a wide variety of country, staying a while in any locality which offers good hunting.

In the 1960s, peregrines suffered a drastic decline in numbers. Prey, such as pigeons, contained toxic residues of pesticides which, accumulating in the peregrine's body, caused either death or infertility. Fortunately some recovery is now taking place but the species is still threatened by egg collectors and falconers wanting young birds or eyasses.

Harriers are slender birds with long, slightly angled wings which are not as pointed as in falcons. Their flight cannot be described as dashing since it

Above: *Hen Harrier* ($\times\frac{1}{4}$). **Above right:** *Golden Eagle* ($\times\frac{1}{8}$).

takes the form of a few leisurely wing beats followed by a glide on partially raised wings at a few feet above open country. When hunting, they quarter an area in this way, scrutinising the ground for prey which is seized by a sudden pounce. They feed largely on small birds and mammals.

In Britain, the Hen Harrier is characteristic of moorland. The cock is ash-grey in colour with black wing tips and a conspicuous white patch on the rump. This last feature, together with the absence of a black bar on the wing, distinguish it from Montagu's Harrier. The females of the two species are more difficult to separate. Both are brown above whilst the under-parts are buff with darker streaks. Each has a light rump patch, said to be purer in the hen harrier, but this is a feature difficult to discern in the field.

Eggs are laid in a simple nest on the ground and incubated by the female.

In pre-war years, the hen harrier was almost confined to the Orkneys and a few Scottish islands. Fortunately it has staged a recovery and now occurs in pockets as far south as the Borders and the northern Pennines. Although many birds are resident throughout the year, some, especially juveniles, move southwards to winter by coastal marshes and dunes.

Until 1939, the Golden Eagle was regarded as being confined to the Scottish Highlands and Western Isles, but since the war a few pairs have become established in south-west Scotland and one pair in the English Lake District.

An eagle's flight is majestic; the wing beats are slow and deliberate, but there are long spells of soaring and gliding on broad wings, the ends of the flight feathers separated and curving upwards. From below it is not unlike a buzzard but it can be recognised by its size, its wing span of six or seven feet being half as big again as a buzzard's, and the head projects further forward, terminating in a huge beak. Adult eagles are uniformly brown in colour except for a golden tinge on the head.

Whereas falcons take prey in the air, the golden eagle tends to beat low over the ground, driving its quarry before swooping to make a kill. In this way it takes hares, rabbits, deer calves, grouse and ptarmigan.

Golden eagles usually breed on cliff ledges, rarely in trees. Nesting sites are often traditional and a pair of birds may have two, using each in alternate years. The nest or eyrie is a bulky structure of twigs or heather, lined with grass and often ornamented with fresh greenery. Normally two eggs are laid early in April and it is some six or seven weeks before they hatch. Chicks are fed at the nest for at least eleven weeks but very often only one youngster survives.

Before 1800, the Buzzard was common throughout mainland Britain. During the nineteenth century there was a gradual decline in numbers, and by the end of the period the bird had disappeared as a breeding species from the east, being largely confined to the bleaker parts of the West

Country, Wales, the Lake District and Scotland.

Buzzards feed on small mammals such as rabbits. These were abundant in many parts of western Britain in the first half of this century, so that by 1954 peak numbers had been attained. Myxomatosis then decimated the rabbit population and, inevitably, buzzards suffered, their numbers falling sharply. Fortunately there has been a gradual recovery so that a circling buzzard is a familiar sight in the sky over desolate moorland or hill country. It soars effortlessly on rounded wings. The plumage is dark brown above and though the under-parts vary in colour, from below the faint barring on the tail is a reliable diagnostic feature.

In the hills, substantial nests are built on rocky ledges and eggs are laid about the end of April, the young being on the wing in July. Although some dispersal of young birds occurs in the autumn, the adults are resident.

Amongst the mountains, the Raven represents the crow family. Totally black in colour, the massive bill and wedge-shaped tail are special features which, together with its size, differentiates it from its fellows. Traversing valleys with measured wing beats it utters abrupt and guttural croaks, 'pruk,

Above left: *Buzzard* ($\times\frac{1}{6}$). **Above:** *Raven* ($\times\frac{1}{6}$).

pruk'. Sometimes it soars in the sky and, whilst doing so in the early part of the year, displays with complicated rolls and dives.

Ravens feed largely on carrion. The species is widely distributed in the northern hemisphere and, in many places, acts like a vulture as a scavenger. In Britain, under pressure, it has retreated to wild hill country and there supplements its diet by killing small animals, especially if they are weak or injured.

Ravens are said to pair for life and often use the same nesting site for several years. Usually the nest is placed on a cliff ledge and is constructed of sticks and earth, lined with moss and wool. It is a robust structure appropriate to its wild situation. Clutches are normally completed in March, incubated for about three weeks and the young are flying some six or seven weeks later. Most ravens are resident throughout the year and family parties stay together until the autumn. Hard weather may cause temporary movements in winter.

Carrion Crows are present at lower levels over moorland. Black in colour like ravens, they are much less bulky, being only half the weight. Their beaks are more slender and the end of the tail is straight rather than bluntly pointed. Their usual call is a hard, resonant 'kraar'. The flight is direct and they do not exhibit the complicated aerobatics of soaring ravens.

As the name implies, a carrion crow will feed on dead carcases but it is also a great robber of nests which makes it extremely unpopular with gamekeepers. Where it is not rigorously controlled it is very common because it has few natural enemies. It is widespread in England and Wales, generally nesting in tall trees, but on moorland where a tree of any size is a rarity, it utilises some isolated crag or stunted bush in hillside scrub.

In Ireland and northern Scotland, the carrion crow is largely replaced by the closely related Hooded Crow in which the back, breast and belly are light grey in colour. Otherwise the two birds are almost identical in form and habits. They are in fact different varieties of the same species and where their ranges overlap, as for example in Inverness, they interbreed and hybrids are common.

Of the other members of the crow family, small communities of Jackdaws sometimes nest amongst crags at intermediate elevations.

Divers may be included with moorland and mountain birds since they are summer visitors to freshwater lochs set in the Scottish Highlands and Islands. Two species are regular breeders, the Black-throated and the Red-throated, and on the mainland are most concentrated in the north-west, with a very small number established below the Clyde.

Divers are well adapted for aquatic life. Their webbed feet are set further back than in other birds, a position which allows them to develop great thrust both on and below the surface of the water, but places them at a disadvantage on land where they can only be described as clumsy. A very

Right: *Black-throated Diver* ($\times \frac{1}{5}$).

short tail terminates a streamlined body which facilitates movement under water. Needless to say, they feed largely on fish and other aquatic creatures.

In Britain the birds are at the southern limit of their breeding range, being typical of northern latitudes in both the Old and New Worlds. Occurring in arctic North America, they are known as loons because of their weird mating calls, a mixed repertoire of mournful wails and sinister gurgling laughs.

The Black-throated Diver derives its name from the black patch on the front of the neck which, in spring and summer, stands out in relief from the black and white striped lateral areas and breast. The dark patch and stripes disappear in winter. It is a large bird, about 2 ft in length, and before becoming airborne is obliged, as might be expected, to gather speed by pattering over the surface of the water. It is normally found on the larger and deeper lochs where it both breeds and feeds. The nest is a simple scrape on an islet, or occasionally on the shore, not far from the water's edge. Two eggs are laid early in May and soon after hatching the young take to the water where they are tended and fed by both parents for about two months. The winter is spent at sea, usually in coastal waters.

Red-throated Divers are smaller and more numerous than black-throats. Being smaller birds, they are capable of rising without difficulty from quite restricted stretches of water and are often found nesting on the margins of small lochans which, though adequate as nesting sites, cannot satisfy a diver's appetite. So they flight to the sea or to larger lochs for fishing. Re-

Above: *Red-throated Diver* ($\times \frac{1}{5}$).

turning, they strike the water breast first, like grebes, rather than with the feet in the manner of ducks.

The red colour of the neck vanishes in winter but at all seasons the slender uptilted bill is a reliable and unmistakable feature.

The breeding cycle of the two species is similar except that the red-throat starts to nest two or three weeks later. In winter the birds are at sea, often forming small flocks on inshore waters.

Moorland tarns and lochs also attract other birds. Gulleries often develop around remote stretches of water, colonies of Black-headed Gulls, sometimes of immense size, being by far the most frequent. Common Gulls congregate in smaller groups with solitary pairs nesting away from open water on boggy moors.

Not surprisingly, ducks also breed in the vicinity. Mallard and, especially in the north, Teal are common but some tracts of moorland hold rarer species. Very small numbers of Common Scoters nest by small lochs in northern Scotland. Wigeon are slightly more numerous, yet apart from a small population in north-west Yorkshire, they are, once again, confined to Scotland.

Finally, on moorland, there are a few native Greylag Geese in the Outer Hebrides and the extreme north of Scotland. Introduced or feral flocks exist elsewhere.